THE CHALICE & THE HEART

by
Gwendolyn Awen Jones

First Paper Back Edition 2007

Published by Angels of Light and Healing
100 South Sunrise Way #302, Palm Springs CA 92262
www.angelsoflightandhealing.org

Book illustrations, photography, text and design © Gwendolyn Awen Jones 2007
The original black and white drawing that inspired this book:
The schema of the archetypal relationship between man and cosmos © Keith Critchlow
was first published 1982 in his book *Time Stands Still*.
Paintings by Leonardo Da Vinci, Dante Gabriel Rossetti and Arthur Hughes.
Stained glass window of Sir Galahad © The Sword in the Stone Ltd.
Courtesy of King Arthur's Great Halls, Tintagel, England.

ISBN 978-0-9740730-2-6
Printed in the USA

Dedicated to all who seek
the Holy Grail

Over the centuries
people have sought the Holy Grail

The Holy Grail is said to be the Chalice
that Christ used in the Last Supper.

The Last Supper

painting by Leonardo Da Vinci

Many believe it was taken to Glastonbury
in England by the uncle of Jesus, Joseph
of Arimathea, after the resurrection.

Glastonbury Tor

There is a protected thorn tree on Wearyall Hill in Glastonbury which is said to have been planted by Joseph of Arimathea.

Tradition states that Joseph thrust his wooden staff into the ground and it immediately flowered. The genus of this thorn tree is found in the Holy Land. It is not native to Britain.

Wearyall Hill seen from Glastonbury Tor

Tradition also suggests that the Holy Grail had a connection to the Chalice Well in Glastonbury. This is an ancient sacred well of healing water.

Some say the Grail was once hidden in the notch in the wall of the well.

Chalice Well, Glastonbury

In the days of King Arthur the twelve
knights of the round table set off on a
quest to find the Holy Grail.

Sir Galahad

painting by Arthur Hughes 1852-1915

Each knight agreed he would take the journey alone and each went in a different direction.

They chose to enter the forest at the darkest points where no paths lay, as they knew if a path existed then it could not be their path.

Adderstone, North Yorkshire

They knew that each individual journey
was a sacred quest where none had gone
before. It was an inner journey.

Knight   *Stained Glass Window,* Tintagel Church

Sir Percival came to the castle of the Fisher King. The King had wounds from a mysterious spell that affected him spiritually and physically, and all his lands lay dying.

The spell could only be broken if certain questions were asked of the King. Percival did not know to ask the questions nor did he recognize the Holy Grail as it passed before him in a procession.

It was not until he had left the castle that he realized his error, but he could never find the castle again.

He spent his whole life trying to go back to it.

Sometimes sacred knowledge passes right before our eyes but we fail to see it either because our consciousness is not prepared or because world affairs distract us.

It was Sir Galahad who found the Holy
Grail. He was the son of Sir Lancelot.

Galahad was the purest of all the knights
and untouched by worldly affairs.

Detail of Sir Galahad receiving the Sanct Grael   Dante Gabriel Rossetti

He was able to enter the sacred sanctuary of his heart and there find his connection to the Holy Grail...

...and through that Holy inner communion his link to the Divine Source.

Sir Galahad receiving the Holy Grail King Arthur's Great Halls, Tintagel

Though the Holy Grail from the Last Supper may be hidden somewhere on the physical plane, it represents the Chalice of the Soul.

The "wine" is the Holy Spirit as it pours into the Chalice.

The journey that each of us needs to make is the inner search for the Divine Source of all life. It requires inner calm, silence, faith and fortitude to face the internal dragons and the external distractions.

The path through the dark forest represents the path to resolve all your lifetimes of un-finished business, hurts and hidden fears.

It is your path towards the Light of the Source and it is your destiny to succeed.

Create a sacred space in which to do your inner work.

Begin the inner journey with prayers to cleanse your mind, body and Spirit.

The journey so far has taken you life-times. It may take many more, or years, or days, or hours....

...it may even happen in a split second in the company of an illumined master, but it will take a special key...

...without the purest love in your heart and a true desire to know the Source, it is impossible to find the Chalice of the Soul or consciously receive the Divine Light.

It begins in the heart...
...as a desire to know

...it requires a pure heart...and a desire to love and to serve the Light to the highest of your potential.

All levels of your being need to be brought under the conscious control of your Higher Self.

This first circle connects your root chakra
with your heart.

It is centered on the solar plexus, the place
of ego and lower will.

This circle also contains the sacral chakra.

The second circle is centered upon your heart chakra – the central point of your inner self – and connects the solar plexus to the throat center.

The third circle, centered upon your throat chakra, connects your heart to your crown and also contains the third eye.

This circle is the place of the higher will and intellect.

The three circles are contained in one. This larger circle represents the sphere of your individualized Being and is centered upon your heart.

Another circle is added, centered upon your root chakra connecting your heart to the sphere of Earth.

You are a part of the Earthly Realm.

The third circle in this group represents the sphere of Heaven and is centered upon your crown chakra.

This is your bridge to the Heavenly Realms.

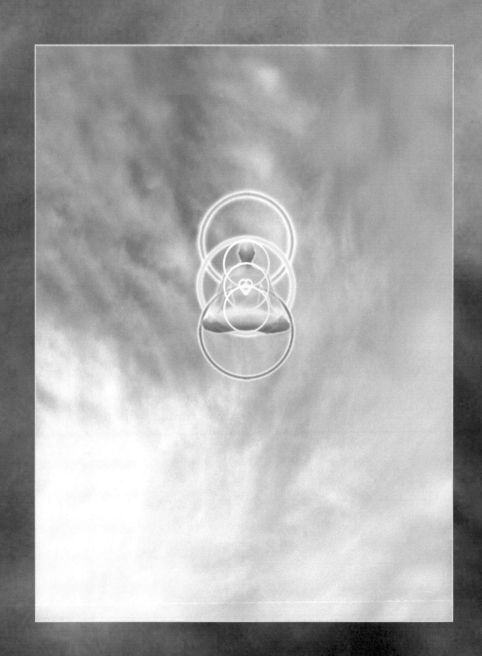

The outer circle is the realm of your Soul. It encompasses all the experiences of your individualized Being in the Heavenly and Earthly Realms.

The heart of your Higher Self – the Spiritual aspect of your Being – sits atop the sphere of the Soul providing the link to your Divine Source.

Through the heart of your Higher Self
you may connect to the Angelic Worlds.

By consciously aligning your physical heart with love and gratitude to the heart of your Higher Self you may begin to open the Chalice of your Soul.

As the Chalice opens
link your heart with love
to the Spiritual center of Mother Earth.

Then connect with love
and reverence to the sphere
of your Higher Self and your contact
with the Divine.

With deep appreciation and thanks
open your heart to the
loving Heart of Mother Earth.

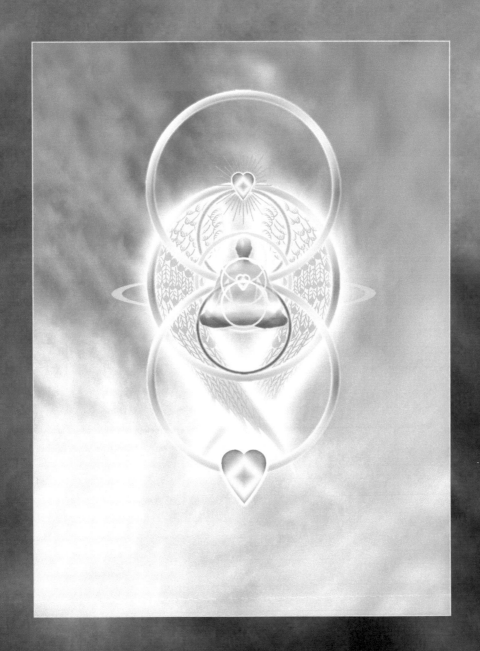

Then in love, joy and with utmost
gratitude, open your heart to the
ever-loving Heart of the
Divine Source.

Within the sphere of Creation
all hearts are now linked in perfect
harmony through your physical heart.

The Chalice represents
your receptive and open Soul
ready to receive the Divine Light.

Slowly breathe the Light of Love
from the Heart of Mother Earth

through your physical heart

to your Higher Self heart

...and then to the Heart of God.

Then gently breathe the Light of Love
from the Heart of the Divine Source

through the heart of your Higher Self
and your physical heart

back to Mother Earth.

Continue this cycle,

...breathing slowly and deeply...

...allowing the Light to fill your whole
Being with each breath.

As the Chalice of your Soul
fills with Divine Light and Love,
all hearts become as One
in Divine Union
within your physical heart.

Then a beautiful Angel
may come to you in a vision,
holding the Golden Grail,
and give you the Sacred Wine
of the Holy Spirit to drink.

When you drink of this Cup
you are One with all Creation
and you understand the hidden
secrets of the Holy Grail.

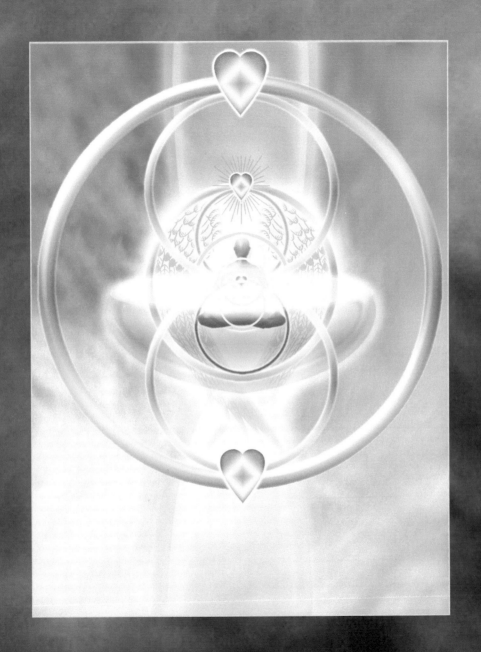

Deep in the Cosmic Void you may find you are not alone but part of a greater mystery.

As your heart links with the Divine, so you awaken the Greater Human Soul out of the depths of ignorance and fear to a higher awareness.

Though we are separate individualized beings, we are all One at the highest levels.

As you reach for the Highest Light, so you raise the consciousness of all Human Kind.

Seek the Holy Grail.

It is your destiny.

About this book – from the author:
In March 2007 as I was researching information on ancient sites in Great Britain to accompany my photographs for my lecture *Paths of Light*, I came across a small black and white line drawing in the book *Time Stands Still* by Keith Critchlow. Though the drawing was small it caught my attention. Having heard Keith speak many years ago in England, I knew he used sacred geometry to express the deepest wisdom. That simple line drawing – a meditating figure with three interlocking circles enclosed within one larger circle – became the basis for this book and my lecture *The Chalice and the Heart*. Keith had given one clue: the circles could be used to create the Kabbalistic Tree of Life. I found over the next two weeks pieces began to fall into place on how it all fit together. In meditation, and even while driving I would get the next image in the sequence in a flash of inspiration. This is my interpretation of the drawing and how it inspired me. My deep gratitude goes to Keith for all his work in keeping the sacred flame alive in the hearts of many generations. There is a lot more hidden in these images for those with the desire to meditate upon them. As the Chalice fills with Light see all hearts become unified into One in your heart. May this lead you to Divine Understanding and the experience of the Holy Grail.
Many Blessings to you on your sacred journey.
Gwendolyn Awen Jones
Full Moon May 31st 2007

About the author:

Gwendolyn Awen Jones is an award winning author, spiritual healer and published artist. She is a medical intuitive and can see all the levels of the human field up to the God connection. In her work as a healer she has found that people need a guide to help them stay in grace after healing work has been done. This book is designed by her as a visual map to the Divine Source. Use it as a meditation tool to stay in alignment with all levels of your Being and the connection to your Source.

Other books by the author:
A Cry from the Womb - Healing the Heart of the World - A guide to healing and helping Souls return to the Light after sudden death, miscarriage, stillbirth or abortion.
This book won the Silver Nautilus Award in 2005

The Angels' Guide to Forgiveness

The Angels' Guide Book to Living on Earth

This book was developed as part of the Angel University Lecture Series.
Due to numerous requests, a poster is available of the final Chalice image on page 77.
For more information on the poster, books, art and lectures by Gwendolyn contact:

Gwendolyn Awen Jones,
Angels of Light and Healing,
100 South Sunrise Way #302,
Palm Springs CA 92262
or go to her web site: www.angelsoflightandhealing.org
e-mail: gwen@angelsoflightandhealing.org

CPSIA information can be obtained
at www.ICGtesting.com
Printed in the USA
LVIW010257060712

2916LVUK00002B

9 780974 073026